What Is ADHD And Is It Contagious?

Attention Deficit Hyperactivity Disorder

And

What You Need To Know About It

Amy Skalicky

Table of Contents

"I'm not random. You just can't think as fast as me."

"I have more thoughts before breakfast than most people have all day."

"I'm sorry...I wasn't paying attention to what I was thinking."

"My ADHD makes it hard for me to focus and focus sounds like hocus pocus and I really like magic a whole whole lot. Abracadabra."

"They say I have ADHD oh look a squirrel!"

We've all seen them—catchy one-liners that make us chuckle upon reading them and become part of a collection of quotes on a Pinterest board. We read them in passing and then move on, never really realizing the hidden truth found in each one. Sometimes, we run across the occasional harmless "I just had an ADHD moment" comment when someone, usually with no experience with ADHD whatsoever, casually quips in response to a forgetful, or "Duh!" moment.

In reality, these charming quotes are illustrative of the world that at least 6% of the world's children and another 6% of adults live in. Although we have known about ADHD for a while, and even have a general idea of what ADHD is, we are still in the age of discovering new information and developing a new and clearer understanding of the disorder, as well as how to not only treat it better, but to manage it more successfully. Thoughts that race around the world twice in two minutes, random ideas that plague the mind at the precise moment directions to an assignment are being given, a million great ideas for that paper but an inability to take Nike's directive and "Just Do It!" as well as a constant struggle to find the car keys or remember the name of the lady with the funny hair who lives just down the street are just a few of the daily struggles an individual living with ADHD may find themselves in.

My Story

I was the energetic, bright child who was labeled gifted early and I was assigned to the "gifted and talented" classes. This was fine, for a while, because I thought I was just like everyone else in my classes, but then I gradually became aware of differences. For instance, while I was reading the same books they read, I couldn't remember the things they did. It was almost like my books had the same cover, but the contents were exclusive. It dawned on me that I was not understanding or even remembering half of what I was reading, and at that point I knew there was a problem. I never said anything to anyone, however. I worked harder and harder, reading and rereading, to cover for the fact that I was struggling, and then would boast about "how easy that was" the next day. Reading and mathematics became my nemesis subjects, and writing, which flowed easily, became my escape. Journaling let me vent and cry silently, and I made up stories in which I was the girl I wished I could be. Meanwhile, reading continued to be a chore, although I somehow developed some strategies to make it easier, such as taking extensive notes. Even though it was a weakness, I actually enjoyed reading. Math, on the other hand, became increasingly difficult once we passed the basics. Word problems and the abstract concepts of algebra befuddled me and I began cheating to maintain my straight A's. My grades were my one saving grace that kept me from being a total loser, and anything less would only confirm my belief that I was not smart. There was also no way I was going to disappoint my parents.

Somewhere in there I also became aware that my mind was busier than everyone else's. I read a quote one time, that I find funny now, but it also describes what I felt then and still experience, although differently, to this day. The quote read "I have a circus in my brain!" The constant bombardment of thoughts and ideas created noise in my head and made it increasingly harder to basically function on any given day. I had few friends, but I never really understood why, convinced only that was there was something wrong with me. I never could put my finger on it, though, or ever figure out a way around it.

I remember when I became conscious of the fact that I experienced the world differently than the average person. For a long time, I had assumed that everyone thought like I did, and then, when I realized they didn't, I felt lost, embarrassed, misunderstood, and like I didn't belong. It was a mistake that I was "gifted", a fluke that I had done well on the evaluations. The chaos in my brain and the difficulty I had focusing long enough to read and actually comprehend what I just read wasn't normal, after all. I felt stupid and afraid that eventually someone would see right through me and call me a fraud, telling me I wasn't smart enough to be in those classes. I struggled with anxiety that overshadowed any positive self-image I once had, until I was sure that I would simply suffocate one day because of the weight that bore down on me. I was already rather quiet and had always sensed that something about me was different, but it would be a long time before I fully understood.

I was 36 years old when I gave birth to my daughter. She was beautiful, funny, active, precocious, and temperamental. When she was four, a friend of mine, who had the expertise to recognize issues in children, sat down with me one day to share that she thought that my daughter had a sensory disorder and probably ADHD as well. I was dumbfounded. You mean the screaming resistance to socks, teeth brushing, hair brushing, and crowded places, as well as the constant seeking of spinning and swinging activities wasn't what all kids did? You mean she wasn't "normal" after all either? What had I done to my daughter?

I made an appointment with her pediatrician, and, long story short, she was diagnosed with ADHD, sensory disorder and anxiety disorder. I educated myself using every resource possible, and, in the process, realized that I had ADHD as well.

I was stunned, but then...what a relief! I had an explanation, a name that I could research and talk to experts about. I am a master researcher and problem-solver, so I was ecstatic to have direction in my previously unsuccessful quest for answers. My whole life, every thought, every feeling, every frustration, every failure...all of it, suddenly made sense to me.

The Nuts and Bolts of ADHD

Please indulge me on this section, because a basic biology lesson is in order to fully explain just what ADHD is, and why it is not merely a figment of the imagination or, no pun intended, not all in someone's head.

 ADHD is a medically recognized disorder with a well-documented neurobiological and neurochemical basis. ADHD primarily involves the frontal, temporal and prefrontal lobes, located in the front of the brain just behind the forehead, part of the cerebrum, and the corpus callosum in the sub-cortical/striatum areas to which the frontal and prefrontal lobes connect. These regions of the brain house executive and inhibitory function, and whose dysfunction is at the heart of an ADHD diagnosis. The basal ganglia controls voluntary movement and pay an important role in learning skills. They also control our response to reinforcement or rewards, important to cause-and-effect learning as well as if-this-then-that reasoning. The caudate nucleus, part of the basal ganglia, communicates with the cortex, where higher reasoning occurs, and it is specifically in charge of controlling motor skills partly by inhibiting particular behaviors and allowing others. The limbic system includes the amygdala and the hippocampus, as well as the interior parts of the frontal, temporal and prefrontal lobes. The limbic system controls our immediate or automatic responses to our environment. MRI studies, EEG studies and PET scans have conclusively demonstrated that the ADHD brain is less active and functions differently in these key areas. These studies have also shown that brain size in children with ADHD is 3-4% smaller than brain size in children without ADHD.

To further understand the biology of ADHD, it is important to also note the chemical component. The frontal and prefrontal lobe functions are assisted by neurotransmitters (chemical messengers). Two neurotransmitters in particular, dopamine and norepinephrine, are primarily responsible for the neurochemical component of ADHD. When both of these chemicals are not properly regulated, it causes problems. Dopamine is responsible for the ability to learn associatively, (cause-and-effect learning), as well problem-solving, attention to detail, perseverance to complete a task, and working memory. Norepinephrine houses the fight-or-flight response, inhibitory abilities to regulate behavioral and emotional responses, and also directly impacts sustained attention. Both neurotransmitters have a direct relationship with alertness, focus, thought sustainability, effort and motivation. The reduced activity in the frontal and prefrontal lobes, combined with the improper regulation of dopamine and norepinephrine, results in an important part of brain functioning being sluggish and the "stop-and-go" capabilities skewed.

Ok, great. What exactly does that mean?

The observable, identifying symptoms of ADHD are hyperactivity, impulsiveness, and distractibility, beyond what is normally characteristic of children, and to the degree that it interferes with the ability to perform daily activities, or is disruptive. Children diagnosed with ADHD typically struggle with disorganization, difficulty transitioning from one task to another, lack of foresight as well as hindsight, difficulty with social skills and reading social cues, frequently feeling overwhelmed and even angry, and lying, cursing, stealing and blaming others, particularly as the child grows older. They are often described as being driven by a motor or not being able to sit still. Can you now recognize how these earmark characteristics are related to the parts of the brain and chemicals described above?

Martine L. Kutscher, MD, author of several books about ADHD, provides a well-laid-out and comprehensive discussion in *ADHD: Living Without Brakes*. Dr. Kutscher uses straightforward language to provide a complete definition of ADHD, including associated symptoms and behaviors, as well as proven treatment and management strategies. Following is a chart from his book that depicts the effect of ADHD on some of these behaviors in relation to children who do not have ADHD:

Symptom	ADHD Children (%)	Typical Children (%)
Argues with adults	72	21
Blames others for own mistakes	66	17
Acts touchy or easily annoyed	71	20
Swears	40	6
Lies	49	5
Stealing (not involving threats)	50	7

However, there is way more to ADHD than generally meets the eye, or to coin the phrase, it is only the "tip of the iceberg." ADHD has been compared to an iceberg by several experts, and with good reason. The observable characteristics are only the beginning. The list of unobservable, or hidden, characteristics is actually much larger, and only when we consider the entire iceberg do we truly have a glimmer of understanding of what life with ADHD can be like.

A number of versions of the ADHD iceberg are available, and each one depicts both the seen and unseen characteristics of ADHD. The national organization, Children and Adults with Attention Deficit/Hyperactivity Disorder, also known as CHADD, has perhaps the most comprehensive version of the ADHD iceberg, providing the pieces of the ADHD puzzle in one snapshot. It is important to note at this point, that not all individuals struggle with all of the characteristics or symptoms; rather, each person has his own combination of these straits. Some must work to overcome only a few, while many have a long and intricate list of challenges that they face every day. Take a look at some of the symptoms that are commonly represented on the ADHD iceberg on the following pages, and you will see what I mean.

THE TIP OF THE ICEBERG

Obvious ADHD Behaviors

IMPULSIVITY

- Difficulty waiting turn
- Lacks self-control
- Blurts out
- Interrupts
- Tells untruths

HYPERACTIVITY

- Restless
- Fidgets
- Can't sit still
- Runs or climbs a lot
- Always on the go
- Talks a lot
- Intrudes
- Talks back
- Loses temper

INATTENTION

- Disorganized

- Doesn't seem to listen

- Distractible

- Makes careless mistakes

- Loses things

- Doesn't do school work

- Forgetful

- Doesn't follow through

BENEATH THE SURFACE

Not-so-obvious ADHD Behaviors

NEUROTRANSMITTER DEFICITS IMPACT BEHAVIORS

- Reduced brain activity for thinking tasks

2/3 HAVE COEXISTING CONDITIONS

- Anxiety

- Obsessive compulsive

- Depression

- Bipolar

- Substance abuse

- Tourette's

- Oppositional Defiant Disorder

- Conduct disorder

WEAK EXECUTIVE FUNCTIONING

- Working memory and recall
- Activation
- Alertness
- Effort
- Internalizing language
- Controlling emotions
- Complex problem solving

SERIOUS LEARNING PROBLEMS

- Specific learning disabilities
- Difficulty memorizing
- Forgets parent and teacher   requests
- Spelling problems
- Slow math calculation
- Poor written expression
- Poor listening and reading comprehension
- Poor processing

LOW FRUSTRATION TOLERANCE

- Difficulty controlling emotions

- Emotionally reactive
- Short fuse
- Gives up easily
- Speaks/acts before thinking
- Difficulty seeing other's perspective

SLEEP DISTURBANCE

- Restless Sleep
- Difficulty falling and staying asleep
- Difficulty waking up
- Night terrors or bad dreams

CAUSE AND EFFECT LEARNING

- Repeats behavior
- Difficulty managing own behavior
- Lacks hindsight and foresight
- Needs immediate rewards
- Behavior modification difficult

LOW FRUSTRATION TOLERANCE

- Difficulty controlling emotions
- Emotionally reactive

- Short fuse
- Gives up easily
- Speaks/acts before thinking
- Difficulty seeing other's perspective

IMPAIRED SENSE OF TIME

- Often late
- Difficulty planning ahead
- Difficulty with long term projects
- Impatient
- Hates waiting
- Homework takes forever

Causes

Researchers have been able to clearly identify a genetic predisposition to being diagnosed with ADHD. Some experts have concluded that ADHD is the most inheritable disorder of all psychological disorders and mental illnesses. While genetic factors control 75-97% of a person's risk for ADHD, several behavioral and environmental factors have been linked to the development of ADHD as well, including smoking and drinking while pregnant, obstetrical complications, increased lead exposure, as well as exposure to other environmental toxins; however, this research is not as clearly understood as the relationship between genetics and ADHD is.

ADHD Myths and Skepticism

In spite of conclusive research and evidence, such as what have shared so far, produced by the medical, psychological and educational communities, there are skeptics who still cling to the claim that ADHD is not "real." In spite of overwhelming evidence to the contrary, there are those who persist in voicing their opinions that ADHD is just an excuse for people who are lazy or sloppy, or to cover up for ineffective parenting. There are also those who deny the existence of ADHD as an avoidance tactic to escape accepting their own diagnosis or the diagnosis of a loved one, usually their own child. This "sticking the head in the sand" approach is often characterized by statements such as "There's nothing wrong with that boy. He just needs more discipline." Or even "Oh, she's fine. She's just whining...she can do her homework just fine if she would only put her mind to it."

Another myth is the belief that ADHD is caused by bad parenting. It is often easy for others who have no direct experience with ADHD to observe a child's impulsive behavior and assume that the parents "just aren't raising him right." In this case, strict parenting, especially if it involves punishing the child for things he cannot control, actually tends to make ADHD symptoms worse.

Still others believe the myth that children who are given special accommodations, or assistance, usually as part of a 504 Plan or IEP, designed to mitigate the interference with learning that symptoms of ADHD creates, actually have an unfair advantage over other students. In reality, supports such as extra time on tests, assistance with organizing, help with assignments or the use of technology such as PDA's or laptops, are meant to even things as much as possible so that children with ADHD have the same favorable conditions in which to learn and to experience success in school, just as their non-ADHD schoolmates did. Supports, while they certainly do help, however, are not a fool-proof solution. Children with ADHD typically will still put forth more effort to achieve the same successes as children without the disorder.

One other popular myth is the belief that children outgrow ADHD. In reality, more than 70% of the children diagnosed with ADHD will continue to have it throughout adolescence, and 75% of those continue to need manage ADHD symptoms throughout adulthood. The current estimate is that 6% of the adult population has, most of whom are undiagnosed. Of those who do have formal diagnosis, only one in ten actively seeks treatment and management strategies

Many people also believe that ADHD means that someone does not have the ability to pay attention or focus for a sustainable amount of time, and I have read plenty of articles that state this as well. However, this description is not completely accurate.   Why am I delving into semantics at this point? Well, this is the next myth I am going to debunk. There are those who use an observation of a child or adult focusing on certain activities, such as playing a video game or spending hours constructing an elaborate structure out of blocks, scraps of wood, and any other material he can find, as a way of arguing the very existence of ADHD. In reality, the ADHD mind will gravitate towards activities it finds appealing. Remember the discussion of the brain that dealt with the limbic system? The brain's motivation to do many things, such as intentionally focusing on something it does not find inviting, does not work so well. That's why the ADHD brain has a short attention span that is easily diverted—it finds the most interesting thing in the room and hones in on it, much like a raccoon that will make a bee line for a shiny object in an otherwise dull environment. Therefore, a more accurate definition of ADHD would be to say that it is characterized by the **unregulated** ability to pay attention or focus.

Along those same lines, another myth of ADHD is the belief that people with ADHD cannot multitask. Again, this is not completely accurate. In many circumstances, multitasking is not successful; however, each individual is different, will actually multitask better than the average person their ideal situations. For example, Bell, whose story you read earlier, and her daughter do not watch television without doing something else at the same time. Bell will tell you that her daughter will color while a program that she is interested in is on, seemingly paying no mind to the television; however, should you inquire, she can tell you exactly what is going on and even quote material from the program. Like her daughter, Bell will be busy doing something, usually something creative like felting or drawing, while watching television, and she too, knows just what is going on. This example illustrates another critical issue for those diagnosed with ADHD, which is the need for action or movement to concentrate. This need does not mean a person with ADHD has to run or jump around to focus; rather, it means that something has to be busy to engage the mind. This is why we often observe students sitting in class with their feet constantly bouncing, their fingers tapping on desks, or fiddling with other objects. Teachers will note on grade reports or notes home to parents that little Johnny cannot sit still in class and constantly fidgets, and if he would only sit still, he would pay better attention. Wrong! In their book *Fidget to Focus*, Roland Rotz, PhD, and Sarah D. Wright, MS, ACT, discuss the relationship between movement, or fidgeting, and focus. Keeping the hands busy is a great way to free the mind, arousing the sluggish sectors into action. Something as simple as a piece of pipe cleaner or a large eraser to be used as a fidget often makes it easier for a child to focus in reading group.

What are Executive and Inhibitory Functioning, and Why Are They So Important?

Executive function, the set of skills controlling how a person performs essential tasks mentally, organizing, setting goals, strategizing, planning and details. When executive functioning is not well-regulated, a person has diminished self-control and self-regulatory capabilities. This is a large part of the "go" of the "stop-and-go" concept.

Inhibitory functioning keeps behaviors and emotional responses in balance, not to hot and not too cold. When inhibitory functioning is not well-regulated in the brain, the results are impulsiveness, lack of inhibition and difficulties controlling emotions. Inhibition, then, is a large part of the "stop" piece of "stop-and-go."

Martin L. Kutscher, MD, includes a comprehensive and easy-to-understand list, with discussion of each, of executive functions in *ADHD: Living Without Brakes*. It is worth briefly listing the common ones here because, not only do they commonly occur alongside ADHD, they change the face of ADHD on an individual basis, and understanding them helps complete the picture of ADHD. Understanding them provides profound insight into the ADHD mountain that must be climbed each day.

Initiation:
the point between thinking about doing it and doing it.

Self-talk:
otherwise known as "talking to yourself," self-talk is the little voice in your head that helps you work through your problems with words.

Working Memory:
is the ideas that we keep active in our thoughts, often at the same time, and apply them to the moment. For instance, when a child is debating whether or not to do homework now or put it off, he must consider what is going on right now with what has happened in the past, and may even include thoughts of the future, such as plans for the weekend or, further in the future, the goal of attending college.

Foresight and Hindsight:
Cause-and-effect, learning from mistakes, decision-making

Sense of time:
General sensing of how much time has gone by or the time of day

Organization:
Refers to developing and/or maintain in an orderly and manageable fashion

Transitioning:
Stopping on activity and moving on to another

Separating Emotion and Fact:
Every event in our lives has an emotional response

embedded somewhere in it which we can differentiate

Motivation:
Adding emotion to objective concept, such as the excitement associated with getting an A on a test

When executive and inhibitory function are not well-regulated in the brain, a person's ability to perform and benefit from these functions is greatly diminished.

Co-Occurring Diagnosis

To complicate ADHD and treatment further, there is a host of other disorders that tend to accompany ADHD. This makes diagnosis and treatment trickier, and it takes a parent who continuously educates themselves, as well as a skilled professional, to successfully devise a treatment plan and management strategies to help a child with ADHD develop life-long coping skills, hopefully minimizing its impact. The more common ones are as follows:

Oppositional defiant disorder:
Identified in nearly half of all children with ADHD

Conduct Disorder:
Excessive aggression towards animals or other people, occurring in approximately 40% of all children with ADHD

Learning Disabilities:
Approximately 70% of all children with ADHD have some type of learning disability, ranging from problems with sequencing to extremely poor handwriting, or dysgraphia

Anxiety:
Nearly 35% of children with ADHD struggle with anxiety and panic attacks

Obsessive compulsive disorders:
Characterized by recurrent and intrusive obsessive thoughts, and the compulsive actions done in attempts to quiet them. OCD is thought to occur in approximately 30% of children with ADHD

Major depression:
Occurs in anywhere from 15%-75% of children with ADHD, and 47% of adults with ADHD

Bipolar depression:
Characterized by mood cycling between depression and manic episodes, occurring in approximately 16% of children with ADHD

Tics and Tourette's Syndromes (motor and vocal tics):
Occur in 7% of children with ADHD, but interestingly enough, 70% of children with Tourette's also have ADHD.

Asperger's Syndrome:
75% of people with Asperger's also have ADHD

Sensory Integration Dysfunction:
Also called sensory processing disorder, it is the inability to process information received through the senses at normal levels. Sensory input is either processed too much or too little, resulting in either sensory-seeking or sensory avoiding behaviors to compensate

Making the Diagnosis

Below is the official criteria for diagnosing ADHD, current at the writing of this book. The benchmarks are officially identified in the American Psychiatric Association's Diagnostic and Statistical Manual of Mental Disorders (DSM) IV, and will be updated in the newest edition, DSM V, which will be released on May 22, 2013.

DSM-IV Decisive factor for ADHD
I. Either display A or B:

A.   **The individual needs to display a minimum of six symptoms of inattentiveness found below. In addition, the symptom must have been present in that individual for a minimum of six months to a degree that is not appropriate for their developmental level:**

Inattentiveness

1.   *Commonly lacks good attention to detail or has a habit of making mistakes made out of carelessness in their work, at school or other activities*

2.   *Difficulty staying focused on task or during activities of play*

3.   *Regularly has a difficult time listening when the individual is spoken to by another*

4.   *Often has trouble following given instructions and fails to complete chores, schoolwork or workplace duties. This is not due to the individual's inability to*

understand the given directions nor behavior that is belligerent.

5. Difficulty in activities involving organization

6. Does not like, or avoids, those activities that involve a great deal of mental effort needed over a long duration (e.g., homework or work from school).

7. Has a regular habit of losing items that are necessary for tasks and activities. Some examples may include writing utensils, books, assignments from school, toys or tools.

8. Lacks focus and is easily distracted

9. Commonly exhibits a pattern of forgetfulness during daily activities.

B. **The individual needs to display a minimum of six hyperactivity-impulsivity symptoms found below. In addition, the symptom must have been present in that individual for a minimum of six months to a degree that is disruptive and is not appropriate for their developmental level:**

Hyperactivity

1. Is unable to sit still and will often fidget with either his/her feet or

2. Often does not follow directions to stay seated

3. Has a habit of running excessively or climbing even when it is not permitted or appropriate (those in teen or adult years tend to feel restless).

4. *Has difficulty playing or having fun with quietness*
5. *Shows no signs of slowing as if run by a motor*
6. *Commonly talks in excess*

Impulsivity

1. *Cannot reserve him/herself to wait in giving an answer and resorts to blurting an answer*
2. *Has difficulty waiting for his/her turn*
3. *Regularly intrudes or interrupts others (for example, during conversation or while at play)*

II. *Some impairment-causing symptoms were displayed prior to the individual's 7th birthday*
III. *Some impairment resulting from the symptoms are found in two or greater settings (such as at home or work/school)*
IV. *It must be clearly evident that there is clinically significant impairments in school, work or social realms.*
V. *The symptoms appear at times other than during Pervasive Developmental Disorder, Schizophrenia or other Psychotic Disorder. Another mental disorder would not better account for the appearance of these symptoms such as an anxiety disorder, dissociative disorder, anxiety disorder, mood disorder or a personality disorder.*

Based on these uncovered criteria, the identification of three types of ADHD is made possible:

IA. Combined Type: Found when both conditions IB and IA are displayed during the course of the previous six months
IB. Predominantly Inattentive Type: Found when condition IA is displayed however condition IB is not displayed during the course of the previous six months
IC. Predominantly Hyperactive-Impulsive Type: Found when condition IB is displayed yet condition IA is not displayed during the course of the previous six months.

According to the American Psychiatric Association, one purpose of modifying the criteria in the new edition, DSM V, is to provide clarity in recognizing ADHD in adults and to facilitate access to treatment and management. A significant portion of adults struggling with ADHD today grew up in an era when ADHD was considered a childhood disorder that somehow disappeared by adulthood, and the understanding of the very existence of ADHD was in its infancy. Consequently, these adults never benefited from a diagnosis, and never had the opportunity to seek treatment or learn how to manage symptoms to decrease their impact on quality of life. These undiagnosed adults struggled with unnamed problems for decades, leaving behind them a path riddled with defeat. Job failure and unsuccessful relationships are two of the most common areas where ADHD weaknesses prevail. The current DSM IV does allow for a diagnosis of ADHD in adults, but it is based on the criteria for children. The DSM V will more accurately characterize the experiences of adults, and ensures that children with ADHD will be able to continue treatment throughout adulthood. Decades of research and studying children who were diagnosed with ADHD as they transitioned into adulthood made it clear that they symptoms usually must continue to be intentionally managed across the lifespan. The premise that ADHD does not simply disappear when a child grows up was confirmed.

The DSM V eliminates the differentiation between ADD and ADHD. In the updated edition, all criteria fall under ADHD. Other modifications that the APA made include changing the onset of impairing symptoms from 7 to 12, and renaming the three subtypes found in DSM IV to three presentations. A fourth type, or presentation, was added for for restrictive attentive ADHD.

The four presentations of ADHD under the soon-to-be-released DSM V are:

> Combined Presentation
>
> Predominantly Inattentive Presentation
>
> Inattentive Presentation
>
> Predominantly Hyperactive Presentation

The APA also removed Pervasive Development Disorder from the exclusion criteria and modified the initiation of the evaluation process to obtain information about the child from two different sources. Often, data from a parent and school staff, usually the child's primary teacher, provide a well-rounded synopsis of the presenting characteristics across the child's two main environments.

Girls and Boys Are Not the Same

Remember the book "Men Are From Mars, Women Are From Venus"? The overarching principle behind that book was simply that men and women are different—they look different, act different, think different, their brains are different, and, stating the most obvious, they have different parts. In particular, research long ago revealed that the male and female brain is biologically different from each other. Differences in neurotransmission synapses (how neurons communicate with each other), brain structure, pruning, dopamine and estrogen all impact how differently males and females think, communication, express emotion, learn and respond the world around them.

At this point, it may be advisable to refer back to the brief biology lesson at the beginning of this article. Continuing on, the frontal and prefrontal lobes, as well as the corpus callosum, already implicated in ADHD, are smaller in boys. Girls, on the other hand, have larger areas in the basal ganglia and limbic systems, specifically the caudate, hippocampus and pallidum areas, but have smaller amygdala than boys. In addition, dopamine is overproduced in boys, contributing to hyperactivity and stereotypical motor movement or tics. However, pruning, this shedding of cells in the brain that it no longer needs, takes place more efficiently in boys, partially balancing dopamine overproduction and explaining the decrease of the severity of hyperactivity in boys after puberty.

Estrogen is potentially another key player in ADHD and a notable factor in differentiating the presentation of ADHD in girls and boys. Estrogen is produced in both male and female bodies, and contributes to not only the development of sex organs, but also to contributes to a significant increase in dopamine and serotonin-binding sites, positively affecting brain maturation and function. Girls have as much as 3-10% more estrogen than boys, and this may contribute to a lessening of some symptoms in girls. However, estrogen levels drop after puberty and again after menopause, increasing the symptoms of ADHD once again. Think of it as two steps up, one step back.

Another key point to note is the onset of other problems in girls brought on by puberty. Hormonal fluctuations throughout the phases of the menstrual cycle result in an increase in ADHD symptomology. Girls with ADHD are more prone to severe premenstrual mood swings laced with irritability, even rage and depression. While 20-30% of the female population experiences some premenstrual discomfort, this rate and the severity of symptoms is much higher in girls with ADHD.

All of these differences translate into observable differences in girls and boys in general, and further explain how and why ADHD looks different in girls as opposed to boys, and has also made it more difficult to recognize. For instance, consider how girls and boys socialize. Girls' relationships are traditionally more complicated and require more maintenance, relying highly on verbal skills and interaction on more complex levels. Boys relate through shared activities, and may meet on the playground, taking off to play football after only a brief exchange with little conversation thereafter, considering themselves now friends, yet the initiation of a relationship between girls is much more dependent upon social cues and bonding. When you introduce a girl who has difficulties with recognizing and responding to social cues, coupled with a tendency to interrupt or blurt out a comment in the middle of a discussion about something completely different, the social awkwardness is apparent and the girl with ADHD is often viewed as "different". Being branded as different in this respect is not often seen in a good light by girls, and so the potential for friendships for a girl with ADHD not only becomes limited, it erodes at her self-esteem and her ability to feel comfortable in her own skin.

Girls exhibit hyperactivity differently than boys do, as well. For years, ADHD was presumed a predominantly male disorder, hence the classic vision of hyperactivity; however, hyperactivity in ADHD girls manifests itself through excessive talking and emotional excitability. Girls whose hyperactivity is apparent through the traditional rowdy behaviors are labelled as tomboys, and are viewed as being bossy, stubborn, dramatic and controlling.

Surprisingly, perfectionism is another key characteristic of many girls with ADHD, and is a often a notable differentiation between boys and girls. Remember Bell? As an example, the typical boy with ADHD will be aware that he has a big paper due the next day, but, with good intentions, will determine he still has plenty of time to complete the project, choosing to do something else that is much more appealing. Suddenly, bedtime approaches and he draws the conclusion that "It's too late now" and settles down to sleep. A girl with ADHD, however, will realize it is now the night before the big project is due, will panic, and will often stay up until the wee hours of the morning making sure it is complete. She will hand it in on time the next day, and likely will even receive an A on it, but the teacher will never realize it was done at the last minute or that she had to work three times as hard completing it. These girls are often also characterized as "people pleasers," contributing to the drive for perfectionism. While this may lead to success in the elementary grades, it often is not enough once a girl reaches middle school and high school. The material is more complicated, for one thing, and the students change classes, inhibiting a teacher's ability to get to know her students. In addition, the social pressures are more demanding, intensifying the feelings of inadequacy, isolation and self-esteem. Girls with ADHD tend to be naïve and too trusting while also struggling with a sense of belonging. In the effort to fit it in, at this point a girl with ADHD is at higher risk to engage in such behaviors as substance use and abuse, sex, and even criminal activity.

Harvard Medical School released a report in 2007 from a study involving girls with ADHD and the prevalence of eating disorders in this segment of the population. The study revealed that ADHD girls are at a higher risk for developing eating disorders. University of Virginia researchers were able to narrow it down in 2008 to a specific eating disorder, bulimia nervosa, or bulimia. Bulimia is characterized by binge-eating and then purging, usually by inducing vomiting or taking excessive amounts of laxatives. The health problems associated with this behavior can be quite serious, resulting in malnutrition, stomach ulcers, tooth decay, hair loss, irregular menstrual cycles, depleted potassium levels, irregular heart rhythms and even death.

Other behaviors that are commonly exhibited in girls with ADHD are daydreaming, being withdrawn, anxious and depressed, as well as picking at her nails and cuticles often, appearing to be silly or show-offish, shyness, inattentiveness, and extra effort to hyperfocus to compensate for other difficulties.

Contributing to the prevalence of underdiagnosed girls with ADHD is the response that teachers often have when a girls exhibits the signs of ADHD. While a boy more often is referred for evaluation and subsequently treatment, a girl is often termed as lazy, "not as far along" as the other children in her class, and is more likely to repeat a grade. This compounds already problematic issues such depression, anxiety and self-esteem. The need for a better understanding of gender differences in ADHD is paramount to providing girls with a successful diagnosis, treatment and a positive long term prognosis. The different presentation of ADHD in girls, however, has only recently become a priority, and there is much more to be understood. It is through research and the willingness of women with ADHD who suffered through childhood without a diagnosis, feeling misunderstood and lost, to share their stories, that the complete picture is unfolding and there is now hope and promise on the horizon.

Management and Treatment: Is There A Cure?

Treatment and management starts with you, the parent, and success will depend largely on your relationships with the other people involved in the care and wellbeing of your child, such as your child's doctor, counselor and teachers. A solid partnership is needed so that all parties are communicating and working together for the same goal. You are your child's teacher, leader, coach, advocate, encourager and rock. He will respond based on your cues.

There are some simple changes a parent can make in the home that will make a big difference to a child with ADHD. Routines and schedules are proven to be very successful in providing needed safety that comes with structure and predictability. Organizing the household environment with places for homework, shoes, toys, jackets and other belongings reduces stress on you and your child, and teaches the value of "everything in its place."

Support groups are a valuable resource for you and your child. Such groups are a great resource for information, resources, practical tips and connecting with other parents striving to support their children with ADHD. Groups for children are also becoming more common, and the benefits of the added support through the connection with peers are high.

It is important to factually educate children about ADHD and what it means for them. Remember, ADHD brings many gifts to the table. Keep the positives on the table along with the challenges. Summer camps developed especially for children with the diagnosis are useful and fun ways to increase children's support structure, and, like support groups, offer tremendous value by providing the opportunity for ADHD children to spend time with their peers as well as opportunities to learn how to better manage the disorder. Summer camps geared toward ADHD needs also provide a foundation for building social skills, self-esteem and much-needed friendships.

While structure is important, it is also important as a parent to loosen up on some things and to pick your battles. Children expend high amounts of energy in making it through any given day, and sometimes they need a break. They aren't going to get it all right on the first try, or the tenth or even the hundredth. Remember the memory impairment? Time and repetition-lots of repetition-are needed for many habits and concepts to make it to the long term memory bank. Patience and forgiveness, and consistency, are way more important than scolding a child for not putting his dirty shirt in the laundry this morning. Keep in mind that however frustrated you may feel, your child not only senses it, but probably feels the same way times ten.

Positive reinforcement is proven to be more effective than negative reinforcement, and it's more fun for parents and teachers, as well as children. If you lack ideas, visit any one of the many reliable resources on the internet, locate a support group, talk to your child's teacher or check out a few books from the library on the subject.

I occasionally catch an article or a blog comment that poses the question "When should I tell my child that they have

ADHD?" I repeated this question to Bell, and this is what she had to say:

Children are way more aware and intelligent than we sometimes give them credit for. A child with ADHD has known for some time that something was different. After the overheard snippets of conversations held with friends, family members, doctors, and teachers, as well as the evaluations and doctor's visits, the child is very clear that something is up, and may actually be anticipating the worse. Kids know when they are being lied to, and it is not the example we want to set for our children. Children respond better when they are respected and included in the very thing that is about them anyway. If you act like it's a tragedy, so will they. If you are positive, supportive, clear that there is nothing "wrong with them" and that they have done nothing wrong, they will respond accordingly. Personally, I find tremendous value in being straight up with my daughter, age appropriately, and teaching her about ADHD, the challenges and the gifts, and including her in problem-solving. Including children in finding solutions communicates to them that they are valued and loved, and it creates much better buy-in than simply being told that this is what is going to happen. Quite frankly, kids sometimes come up with much better and more creative solutions, and while an idea may be proposed that is perhaps not ideal from your perspective, if it works and is not harmful, what's wrong with the compromise? The empowerment a child feels after having a part in the decision-making and having his idea be the answer, is invaluable and the returns come back ten-fold. We, as adults, don't always have to be right, because goodness knows we aren't.

While some are tempted to say "No, way!" when broached with the possibility of using medication as part of a treatment plan, it is important to stop and consider a few things. First, how much do you really know about the various medications used to treat ADHD symptoms? There is a plethora of misinformation available from many sources, including the internet, so talk with your child's doctor and locate a few reliable sources of information for research. Medication does not work well for everybody, and initially dosage must be tweaked a few times to find success. Make sure you are fully informed before making a decision.

Medication does not cure ADHD, and it does not treat all symptoms. The medications prescribed today are designed to "wake up" the parts of the brain that are underactive so that key functions are improved and a foundation is laid to implement other treatment and management strategies. It is important to note here that the brain is a muscle that can be worked out and developed, just as the other muscles can be developed and functionality improved. This is also known as neuroplasticity. Counseling, behavioral and cognitive therapy, social skills training, learning organizational techniques, and overall learning, are not only proven to be successful, they are more successful when the brain is chemically balanced.

Dr. Kutscher discusses ADHD medications in *ADHD: Living Without Brakes,* and in it he states that, in patients where medication is successful, children do not feel different on medication, they only perform differently. When asked, children are aware that they are doing certain things better. If medication does not provide an improvement in certain symptoms, namely, the ability to pay attention, creates side effects that are not tolerable or pose a health risk, or if it does create a "different feeling", the chances are the medication is not the right choice and a different one may be tried, the dosage adjusted, or discontinued all together.

The risks of not being on medication when warranted to help bring ADHD under control are also clearly noted by Dr. Kutscher. He reminds us that without proper medication when indicated, children with ADHD are at a 30% higher risk for substance abuse, a very high risk for dropping out of school, develop significantly diminished self-esteem, which carries its own set of risk factors, and are at a significantly greater risk for automobile accidents.

There is a menu of evidence-based and proven methods for treating and managing ADHD in addition to medication. While all of them will not be appropriate or successful for everyone, one or two can usually be easily identified that produce positive results. Three key management areas are universal to anyone diagnosed with ADHD. They are:

> **Sleep**: sleep problems are sometimes associated with ADHD, which only exacerbates symptoms. Sleep management is made easier by getting plenty of exercise during the day, creating a bedtime routine that incorporates relaxing activities such as a warm bath, a health snack, bed time stories, a back massage or listening to relaxing music or nature sounds, such as the sound of rain falling. Avoid television and sugar late in the evening.

Diet: While a poor diet does not cause ADHD, some elements of an unbalanced diet can make symptoms works. Consider reducing processed sugar and certain food dyes, primarily reds and yellows.

Exercise: Exercise increases neurotransmitters connected with ADHD, namely dopamine and norepinephrine (remember them?), and releases energy, important especially to children diagnosed with the hyperactive ADHD.

Children diagnosed with ADHD also benefit from learning to use various tools as part of a management strategy. Simple methods such as creating to-do lists, writing things down in a notebook that is always kept handy, using a voice recorder to supplement note taking in class, the use of calendars and planners, and using timers to schedule work activities and breaks, are all proven to be successful uses of tools for ADHD management. Remember, a diagnosis of ADHD is not the end of the story; rather, it is simply the beginning of a different and interesting chapter.

.

ADHD...A Gift?

"In my opinion, ADHD is a terrible term. As I see it, ADHD is neither a disorder, nor is there a deficit of attention. I see ADHD as a trait, not a disability. When it is managed properly, it can become a huge asset in one's life. I have both ADHD and dyslexia myself and I wrote a book with Catherine Corman, *Positively ADD: Real Success Stories to Inspire Your Dreams*, profiling a collection of fabulously successful adults all of whom have ADHD, so I know whereof I speak. As I like to describe it, having ADHD is like having a powerful race car for a brain, but with bicycle brakes. Treating ADHD is like strengthening your brakes-so you start to win races in your life." These words were spoken by Edward M. Hallowell, MD. He was a graduate of Harvard and Tulane Medical School plus the author of numerous books on ADHD and ADHD coach. He is one of many who have mastered and overcome the art of controlling ADHD's symptoms and he is successful at preventing this disorder from meddling with his goals. Hallowell chose to welcome the various gifts connected with ADHD, saying that attitude has the greatest impact or the outlook one takes, and whether the attitude or the outlook is embraced by the individual determines the success one can have during their journey throughout life. Hallowell declares, "It's how you manage the ADHD that determines whether it's a gift or a curse,". He and Catherine Corman opened up the floor for seventeen people coming from varying backgrounds, who were also engaged in various occupations, including political advisor James Carville, Books-a-Million chairman Clyde Anderson, and the inventor of the e-ticket as well as the CEO of JetBlue, David Neelman, to share their own journeys toward success and leading fulfilling lives. According to Dr. Hallowell, each person who added his voice to the collection did not battle their ADHD on the road to success; rather, they embraced ADHD wholly, challenges and gifts, to create a synergistic existence that capitalized on the disorder's many strengths.

One common trait among individuals who have set goals and attained them is a sense of humor and the ability to laugh at themselves. Bell, whose own story may be added to countless other success volumes, finds humor in ADHD-related quotes she runs into on the internet.

> *Every one of them is so true, and they really crack me up. ADHD and blonde quotes make me laugh...because ADHD is quite comical. Here are three of my favorites:*
>
> *"Without deviation from the norm, progress is not possible." Frank Zappa*
>
> *"Creativity is intelligence having fun." Albert Einstein*
>
> *"I am always ready to learn although I do not always like being taught." Winston Churchill*
>
> *"No one can make you feel inferior without your consent," spoken by Eleanor Roosevelt, although not humorous, is another favorite, for it keeps my perspective healthy.*

Creative, indeed, as evidence backs up the claim that people with ADHD tend to have a high amount of creativity, are exuberant, have profound emotional expressiveness, keen interpersonal intuition, a special relationship with nature, and highly-developed leadership skills. Flourishing imaginations, the phenomenal energy, and an uncanny ability to "think-outside-the-box" makes them particularly adept at problem-solving. They are willing to take risks, which often makes them successful entrepreneurs, artists, musicians and authors.

I have frequently heard people with ADHD say that they know that they notice things in life that escapes those without ADHD, and I think they may just be right. Bell agrees, and shares this with me:

> *At the age of 40, I gained control of my ADHD and stopped letting it control me. I realized that I did, indeed, belong, and that I had my own brand of individuality. I have awesome ideas and creativity, a passion for researching and writing, and a playfulness that allows me to bond with children in a way that many adults don't understand. It finally dawned on me to re-evaluate my career goals, redirecting my pursuits toward endeavors that maximized my strengths. I am now pursuing a career as a freelance writer, and I love it. I also have been able to work with my daughter to teach her about managing symptoms, but allowing yourself to BE YOURSELF! She is "gifted" as well…and THRIVING! I love her creativity, her energy and her beautiful heart that allows her to connect with others. I often receives comments about how mature she is for her age, and I see it too. We will always get through the tough days. ADHD is a blessing in so many ways—high creativity, atypical problem-solving strategies, and being able to say "I understand" to my daughter with complete honesty. I am truly thankful for it.*

In the words of Dr. Zeuss, "Why fit in when you were born to stand out?"

Adult ADHD

The new face of ADHD is the adult face. While there is no cure, those with milder symptoms find that they decrease into adulthood, as the brain fully matures; however, 65% continue with symptoms throughout their adult lives. Interestingly enough, only 1 in 10 adults diagnosed with ADHD actually seek care. Most of these now-adults ceased their medication by high school, with only 5% of those originally started on medication still consistent at the age of 21. These decisions to discontinue treatment are significant decisions that bring adverse consequences throughout adulthood, unless self-awareness inspires individuals to resume support.

Many adults with ADHD discover that they have unknowingly developed coping strategies or ways of compensating for some difficulties.

According to Dr. Ned Hallowell, who has his own child and adult psychiatry practice and is the founder of the Hallowell Center for Cognitive and Emotional Health in Sudbury, Massachusetts. If an adult has displayed a minimum of twelve of the behaviors (found below) since childhood, plus if these symptoms are not correlated with any other diagnosis (medical or psychiatric) then an ADHD official evaluation is a fitting course of action.

- Individual commonly displays a sense of underachievement or inability to meet goals that is unrealistic. It does not even matter how much the individual has accomplished.

- Lacks the ability to become organized and stay organized

- Lacks the ability to jump on tasks and is a chronic procrastinator

- Has many projects going on at one time, yet fails to complete those projects

- Speaks whatever comes to mind yet lacks a filter for what might need filtering

- Has a perpetual need for all things exciting

- Boredom aversion

- Cannot stay focused and is easily distracted, tends to become absent or drift away even while engaged in conversation or in the midst of a page. This is often in addition to focusing difficulties.

- Often imaginative, perceptive, highly intelligent

- Difficulty following a course of action or protocol.

- Becomes easily frustrated and lacks patience

- Impulsive both behaviorally and verbally

- irritability

- Worries in excess and will even give him/herself something to worry about

- Lacks feeling of security

- Temperamental

- Fidgety physically or mentally.

- Personality or behavior that is addictive

- Chronic case of low self-esteem.

- Individual's assessment of self lacks accuracy
- Family history exposes ADHD or other mood disorder

CHADD's Program FAST MINDS

FAST MINDS is an acronym for the daily challenges faced by those living with ADHD. It is a technique designed to shift the focus from external consequences to internal self-exploration. Children, with guidance, as well as adults, benefit from learning to shift from being reactive to being proactive. The following is CHADD's elaboration of the meaning of the acronym:

FORGETFUL:
Do you have a tendency to forget what individuals have told you? Do you lose track of where you have placed items? Do you require reminders for everyday things? Do you forget appointments?

ACHIEVING BELOW POTENTIAL:
Do you feel you underachieve? Do you feel you should be getting better grades than you do at school, or should have made it further than you have in your career?

STUCK:
Are you finding it difficult to get ahead in life? Does it feel as though you are continuously being pushed down as you attempt to stay above water? Are you playing a routine game of catch-up as opposed to enjoying life in the way you desire? Are you finding yourself routinely stuck in life's critical areas like school or work?

TIME CHALLENGED:
Are you perpetually late? Do you find yourself overestimating the amount of time required of various things? Does time drift away? Do you have trouble figuring out how long a task is "supposed" to take?

MOTIVATIONALLY CHALLENGED:
Are you a procrastinator? Do you complete things during the eleventh hour or require deadline pressures in order to accomplish things? Do you have a hard time getting started on tasks? Do you get partway done with many tasks but have trouble completing them?

IMPULSIVE:
Do you do things without anticipating consequences (making decisions, shopping, driving, sex, drugs)? Do you interrupt conversations by blurting things out? Do you participate in risky sexual behavior? Do you make purchases without considering the cost or your budget?

NEW ADVENTURE SEEKER:
Do you find yourself in a perpetual state of boredom? Do you search out experiences that are stimulating and new in order to avoid the rut of boredom? Do you have difficulty saying no to obligations regardless of the busy schedule you are already facing?

DISTRACTIBLE:
Do you find yourself distracted by sounds, thoughts, sights, or activities that are of a lower priority? Are these

distractions keeping you from the course you should be following? Are daydreams a part of your daily routine?

SCATTERED:
Are your personal spaces in a disordered state? Is there disarray in your vehicle, on your desk, or even in your home? Do you have a difficult time staying ahead of what needs to be accomplished and in the timeliness factor that it requires?

Once these questions are thoughtfully answered, the FAST MINDS program encourages people with ADHD to consider times when they felt successful, when circumstances made it possible to perform at their best. The process includes noting what they were doing, where they were, who they were with, what strengths were capitalized upon, and how they felt. Digging into these experiences helps to analyze what made them work and to notice any patterns. Patterns help develop direction, shifting from what does not work to what does, and helps people to use this information to formulate strategies that will improve the overall quality of life and chances for success in the future. Success then repeats. CHADD describes the principles that underlie these strategies:

- Emotional, negative thoughts and distracting environments can be minimized.
- Our brains engage best in interesting, meaningful tasks, with clear steps that can be held in mind.
- Many challenging functions can be outsourced to "peripheral brains" (alarm reminders, smartphones, planners, other people).

- The right habits at the right moment can keep one from falling off track with daily demands, impulsivity, and relationships.
- It takes the right environment—and accountability— to practice new strategies.

CHADD, like other ADHD-specific organizations and resources, provides information and tools to develop personalized management to mitigate ADHD symptoms and improve overall outcomes and quality of life.

It takes time and patience for an individual to sort through information found in articles, websites and books, as well as that gathered from doctors and other subject-matter experts, but the investment lasts a lifetime. While there is no shortage of treatment options, debates over what works and what doesn't, as well as advice, success can be found. It is a process. The time, patience and trial-and-error that it takes to create a plan that works can seem daunting at first, but rather than become overwhelmed, tackle it a little at a time. Remember the old question "How do you eat an elephant?" The answer to that question really is true. You eat that elephant "one bite at a time."

About The Author

Amy Skalicky is a freelance writer with a degree in Communications and masters in General Psychology. A Colorado resident, she has ten years of experience educating and advocating for families and youth with disabilities and special health care needs. As an adult with ADHD, as well as the parent of a child with the same diagnosis, she is well-versed in the challenges and gifts of ADHD, and works to support others striving to rise above it.

Email elephanttreefeatures@gmail.com

my site www.elephanttreefeatures.com

www.ingramcontent.com/pod-product-compliance
Lightning Source LLC
Chambersburg PA
CBHW050825290526
45792CB00001B/270